Provisions on Child Abduction in Non-Hague Countries

East Asia and the Pacific • Europe and Central Asia
Latin America and the Caribbean • Middle East and North Africa
South Asia • Sub-Saharan Africa

May 2015

The Law Library of Congress, Global Legal Research Center
(202) 707-6462 (phone) • (866) 550-0442 (fax) • law@loc.gov • http://www.law.gov

Contents

I. East Asia and the Pacific

II. Europe and Central Asia

III. Latin America and the Caribbean

IV. Middle East and North Africa

V. South Asia

VI. Sub-Saharan Africa

Provisions on Child Abduction in Non-Hague Countries

Staff of the Global Legal Research Center

SUMMARY   This report covers laws on parental child abduction and the legal aid that may be available to parents of abducted children in thirty-eight countries that have not signed the Hague Convention on the Civil Aspects of International Child Abduction.[1] The responses are organized by region of the world: East Asia and the Pacific, Europe and Central Asia, Latin America and the Caribbean, the Middle East and North Africa, South Asia, and Sub-Saharan Africa. While in many countries no specific legislation or programs dealing with international abduction of children could be located, existing laws and general legal aid programs may be relevant.

I. East Asia and the Pacific

Burma (Myanmar)

Burma does not appear to provide legal representation for a parent in a foreign country whose child was abducted and lives in Burma. There is a legal aid system, but it is still being developed.[2]

Burma also does not appear to provide legal representation for a parent whose child was abducted from Burma to a foreign country.

China

Under Chinese law, there are no legal provisions specifically addressing international parental child abduction or legal assistance available for those involved. Free legal assistance is available to Chinese citizens in civil and criminal proceedings, with the scope of cases and eligibility for the aid provided in the nationally applicable Regulations of Legal Aid.[3] Parental child abduction is not a criminal offense. In addition to the requirement of economic difficulty in hiring a representative, the Regulations limit family law cases for which a party may apply for legal aid to disputes over alimony for parents or spouses, and child support payments.[4] Therefore, it is unlikely that individuals involved in international parental child abduction would be eligible for legal aid.

---

[1] Convention of 25 October 1980 on the Civil Aspects of International Child Abduction, Oct. 25, 1980, http://www.hcch.net/index_en.php?act=conventions.text&cid=24.

[2] Liz Riegel, *Assessment Trip to Myanmar – Thanks, 2014 Donors!*, GLOBALGIVING (Mar. 4, 2015), https://www.globalgiving.org/projects/legal-aid-in-post-conflict-countries/updates/.

[3] Falü Yuanzhu Tiaoli [Regulations on Legal Aid] (promulgated by the State Council on July 21, 2003, effective Sept. 1, 2003), FAGUI HUIBIAN 102-107.

[4] *Id.* art. 10.

Indonesia

No specific provisions were located in Indonesian law regarding international parental child abduction or legal assistance for those involved. Under Law No. 16 of 2011 on Legal Aid[5] and Government Regulation No. 42 of 2013,[6] free legal assistance is available for civil proceedings, mediation, and nonlitigation matters. Eligibility is based on a provision in the Law that states that recipients of legal aid include "any person or group of poor people who cannot meet the basic right [sic] appropriately and independently."[7] In addition to a written application, people must provide a letter from the head of village or other official where they live certifying that they are poor. Government legal aid funding is administered by the Ministry of Law and Human Rights, with legal assistance delivered by more than three hundred accredited organizations throughout the country.[8] Mediation services are available through the religious courts,[9] which handle family law cases involving Muslims,[10] as well as the civil courts.[11]

Laos

Laos does not appear to provide legal representation for a parent in a foreign country whose child was abducted and lives in Laos.[12] There is a legal aid system, but it is still being developed.

Laos also does not appear to provide legal representation for a parent whose child was abducted from Laos to a foreign country.

---

[5] Law No. 16 of 2011 on Legal Aid, http://www.setneg.go.id/components/com_perundangan/docviewer.php?id=2824&filename=UU%2016%20Tahun%202011.pdf (in Indonesian).

[6] Government Regulation No. 42 of 2013 on Terms and Procedure for Legal Aid and Legal Assistance Fund Distribution, http://www.ekon.go.id/hukum/download/325/83/pp-42-2013.pdf (in Indonesian). See Press Release, Cabinet Secretariat of the Republic of Indonesia, President Signed the Government Regulation Regarding Free Legal Aid for the Poor (June 10, 203), http://old.setkab.go.id/en/news-8997-president-signed-the-government-regulation-regarding-the-free-legal-aid-for-the-poor.html.

[7] Erna Ratnaningsih, *Legal Aid System in Indonesia* (undated), http://www.unct.org.bt/legalaid/doc/presentations/Legal%20Aid%20System%20in%20Indonesia_ER.ppt (last visited Apr. 22, 2015); Law No. 16 of 2011, art. 5.

[8] Constantinus Kristomo, *New Laws to Provide State-Funded Legal Aid in Indonesia*, INNOVATING JUSTICE FORUM, http://www.innovatingjustice.com/innovations/new-laws-to-provide-state-funded-legal-aid-in-indonesia (last visited Apr. 22, 2015).

[9] *See* The Asia Foundation, *Religious Courts: Improving Women's Access to Justice in Indonesia* (undated), https://asiafoundation.org/resources/pdfs/V4IDReligiousCourtsWEP4pgWEB.pdf (last visited Apr. 22, 2015).

[10] Law No. 7 of 1989 on the Religious Judicature, art. 2, http://www.komisiyudisial.go.id/downlot.php?file=UU%20No%207%20Thn%201989%20PERADILAN%20AGAMA.pdf (in Indonesian).

[11] *See* Supreme Court Regulation No. 1 of 2008 on Court Mediation Procedure, https://www.mahkamahagung.go.id/images/uploaded/prosedur_ttg_mediasi0001.pdf (in Indonesian).

[12] Hiroshi Matsuo, ACCESS TO JUSTICE IN INDOCHINESE COUNTRIES IN INSTITUTIONAL COMPETITION BETWEEN COMMON LAW AND CIVIL LAW: THEORY AND POLICY, 249, 265 (Michèle Schmiegelow ed. 2014).

Malaysia

No specific provisions were located in Malaysian law regarding international parental child abduction or legal assistance for those involved.[13] The Legal Aid Act 1971 provides for legal aid to be granted to eligible applicants involved in civil proceedings,[14] including in relation to "[r]ights and liabilities in respect of proceedings for divorce and custody."[15] It appears that eligibility for legal aid is restricted to persons with annual incomes of less than RM25,000 (about US$6,888), for whom such aid is free, and those with incomes between RM25,000 and RM30,000 (about US$8,265), who must contribute RM300 for their legal costs.[16] Government-funded legal aid for civil cases is administered by the Legal Aid Department, which falls under the Prime Minister's Department. The Legal Aid Department, through various branches, provides advice and representation to clients as well as mediation services.[17]

Mongolia

No provisions directly concerning international parental child abduction under Mongolian law could be found in the English-language sources consulted. Mongolia does have a Family Law, which came into effect on August 1, 1999;[18] some provisions of that law, taken together, could be seen as a basis for requesting assistance from courts or other governmental institutions in cases of child abduction. The Law states that a child's welfare must be respected,[19] that the court must protect the rights of the family,[20] and that state administrative and social welfare institutions must also protect the rights of the family.[21]

The Law also states that divorced parents cannot limit each other in ways that result in there being difficulties in carrying out their duties to their children.[22] It adds that parents have the right to demand the return of a kidnapped child.[23]

---

[13] For analysis of Malaysian laws relevant to international parental child abduction see Suzanna Muhammad Said & Shamsuddin Suhor, *International Parental Child Abduction in Malaysia: Foreign Custody Orders and Related Laws for Incoming Abductions*, 20(S) PERTANIKA J. SOC. SCI. & HUM. 101 (2012), http://www.myjurnal.my/filebank/published_article/16009/9.pdf.

[14] Legal Aid Act 1971 (Act 26), pt 4, http://www.agc.gov.my/Akta/Vol.%201/Act%2026.pdf.

[15] Legal Aid (Amendment to Third Schedule) Order 2011, http://www.federalgazette.agc.gov.my/outputp/pua_2011_1230_PERINTAH%20BANTUAN%20GUAMAN%20%28PINDAAN%20JADUAL%20KETIGA%29%202011.pdf [scroll down to locate text in English].

[16] *Eligibility of the Applicant*, LEGAL AID DEPARTMENT, http://www.jbg.gov.my/index.php?option=com_content&view=article&id=131&Itemid=284&lang=en (last visited Apr. 22, 2015).

[17] *Function*, LEGAL AID DEPARTMENT, http://www.jbg.gov.my/index.php?option=com_content&view=article&id=65&Itemid=216&lang=en (last visited Apr. 22, 2015).

[18] Family Law (June 11, 1999), *available at* http://www.ilo.org/dyn/natlex/docs/ELECTRONIC/57595/105357/F-139350413/MNG57595%20Eng.pdf.

[19] *Id.* art. 4.5.

[20] *Id.* art. 5.1.

[21] *Id.* art. 5.2.

[22] *Id.* art. 26.2.

Mongolia has a government agency devoted to implementing rules on child welfare, the National Authority for Children, which is located in the capital city of Ulan Batar.[24]

Mongolia has a legal aid system that is run by the Mongolian Association of Advocates, a nongovernmental organization. The Association's efforts cover both criminal and civil matters. Assistance is dependent on need in other than the most serious criminal cases; for those serious cases, no means test is applied.[25]

Papua New Guinea

No specific provisions were located in the laws of Papua New Guinea regarding international parental child abduction or legal assistance for those involved. The Public Solicitor, established under the Constitution, is tasked with providing legal aid, advice, and assistance to eligible criminal defendants when directed by the Supreme Court or the National Court and at his or her own discretion in civil and criminal matters.[26] This includes assistance in family law matters.[27] Mediation services are provided by the courts in relation to a range of civil matters.[28]

Philippines

No information was located as to whether the Philippines provides legal assistance to a parent whose child was abducted to or from the country. Also, no information was located indicating whether there is an agency handling legal representation for such parents.

Vietnam

Vietnam has a general legal aid system for particular groups of people, including poor people,[29] but does not appear to provide legal representation for a parent in a foreign country whose child was abducted and lives in Vietnam. Vietnam also does not appear to provide legal representation

---

[23] *Id.* art. 33.1

[24] *Regulatory and Implementing Agencies of the Government of Mongolia*, INFOMONGOLIA.COM, http://www.info mongolia.com/ct/ci/1702/138/Regulatory%20and%20Implementing%20Agencies%20of%20Mongolian%20Govern ment (last visited Apr. 22, 2015).

[25] *Legal Aid in Mongolia*, AMERICAN UNIVERSITY SCHOOL OF PUBLIC AFFAIRS, http://jpo.wrlc.org/bitstream/ handle/11204/3842/Mongolia.pdf?sequence=1 (last visited Apr. 22, 2015).

[26] Constitution of the Independent State of Papua New Guinea § 177(2), http://www.paclii.org/pg/legis/consol act/cotisopng534/.

[27] The Independent State of Papua New Guinea Public Solicitor's Office (PSO), *Public Solicitor's Role in Providing Legal Assistance* (2012), https://elo.legalaid.qld.gov.au/webdocs/dbtextdocs/internal/irregseries/cle/2012/ pngpso.pdf.

[28] *About Civil Cases*, THE SUPREME AND NATIONAL COURTS OF PAPUA NEW GUINEA, http://www.pngjudiciary. gov.pg/home/index.php/national-court/civil-cases (last visited Apr. 22, 2015).

[29] Law No. 69/2006/QH11 (June 29, 2006) Law On Legal Aid art. 10.

for a parent whose child was abducted from Vietnam to a foreign country. Embassies of Vietnam may provide general consular assistance in such cases.[30]

II. Europe and Central Asia

Azerbaijan

According to the Family Code of Azerbaijan, all family-related disputes must be adjudicated by the local district court where one of the spouses permanently resides.[31]

Azerbaijani law does not appear to include any specific provisions regarding international parental child abduction or legal assistance for those involved. The Criminal Code of the Republic of Azerbaijan does not recognize parental abduction as a crime. The only relevant provision of the Criminal Code is article 144.3, which punishes kidnapping of a minor by imprisonment for ten to fifteen years; however, it is not clear if abduction of a child by a parent in violation of custody rules is covered by this Law.[32]

Special procedures exist for minors to cross the national border. According to the Law on Exit from the Country, Entry into the Country, and Passports, a person under the age of eighteen may leave the country with the consent of his/her parents or legal representative, which is certified by a notary. In the absence of consent from one of the parents, the matter of exiting the country must be resolved by a court.[33] For minors traveling abroad for permanent residence, exit from the country is allowed only with the consent of each parent or the child's legal representative.[34]

Kyrgyz Republic

The law of the Kyrgyz Republic does not appear to contain specific provisions regarding international parental child abduction or legal assistance for those involved. The Criminal Code of the Kyrgyz Republic[35] does not recognize parental abduction as a crime. The only relevant provision of the Criminal Code is article 123.3, which punishes kidnapping of a minor by imprisonment for ten to twenty years.[36]

---

[30] Decree No. 15/2008/ND-CP (Feb. 4, 2008) Defining the Functions, Tasks, Powers and Organizational Structure of the Ministry of Foreign Affairs art. 2, item 13 a.

[31] FAMILY CODE OF THE REPUBLIC OF AZERBAIJAN, Law No. 781-IQ, art. 7, Dec. 28, 1999, http://www.taxes.gov. az/uploads/qanun/2011/mecelleler/aile_mecellesi_rus.pdf (in Russian).

[32] CRIMINAL CODE OF THE REPUBLIC OF AZERBAIJAN, No.787-IQ, art.144.3, Dec. 30, 1999, *available at* http://www. legislationline.org/download/action/download/id/1658/file/4b3ff87c005675cfd74058077132.htm/preview.

[33] Law on Exit from the Country, Entry into the Country, and Passports, No. 813, art. 2, June 14, 1994, http://www. migration.gov.az/images/pdf/aa536a87842307ede34f4b8fd59fa885.pdf.

[34] *Id.*

[35] CRIMINAL CODE OF THE KYRGYZ REPUBLIC, Law No. 69, Oct. 1, 1997, *available at* http://www.legislationline. org/ documents/section/criminal-codes.

[36] *Id.* art. 123.3.

Special procedures must be followed when a minor is crossing the national border. According to the Law of the Kyrgyz Republic on External Migration, a person under the age of eighteen may exit the country upon the request of his/her legal representatives. Such requests must be certified by a notary. The exit of a minor may also be authorized by a court decision in the absence of an agreement between the child's legal representatives.[37] The exit of a minor aged fourteen to eighteen years to a foreign country for permanent residence is allowed only with the written consent of the child's legal representative, certified by a notary.[38]

Liechtenstein

While Liechtenstein is not a party to the Hague Convention on the Civil Aspects of International Child Abduction, it is a party to a comparable regional convention, the European Convention on Recognition and Enforcement of Decisions concerning Custody of Children and on Restoration of Custody of Children (European Convention),[39] which entered into force for Liechtenstein on August 1, 1997.[40] That Convention addresses the "improper removal" of a child, defined as "the removal of a child across an international frontier in breach of a decision relating to his custody which has been given in a Contracting State and which is enforceable in such a State."

Article 2 of the European Convention provides that each contracting state must appoint a central authority to carry out the functions provided for by the convention. The government of the Principality of Liechtenstein was designated as the central authority according to article 2.[41]

Liechtenstein is also a party to the Convention on the Rights of the Child (CRC),[42] which contains provisions relevant to international child abduction. Article 11, paragraph 1 of the CRC postulates that State Parties must take measures to combat the illicit transfer and non-return of children abroad. In order to implement the CRC, Liechtenstein enacted the Act on Children and Adolescents (Kinder- und Jugendgesetz, KJG).[43] The Office of Social Affairs (Amt für Soziale

---

[37] Law on External Migration, No. 61, art. 40, July 17, 2000, *available at* http://www.legislationline.org/ documents/ action/popup/id/4978.

[38] *Id.*

[39] Council of Europe, European Convention on Recognition and Enforcement of Decisions Concerning Custody of Children and on Restoration of Custody of Children (European Convention), COUNCIL OF EUROPE TREATY SERIES [CETS] No. 105 (May 20, 1980).

[40] Europäisches Übereinkommen über die Anerkennung und Vollstreckung von Entscheidungen über das Sorgerecht für Kinder und die Wiederherstellung des Sorgerechts [European Convention on Recognition and Enforcement of Decisions concerning Custody of Children and on Restoration of Custody of Children] [European Convention], LGBL 1997, No. 110.

[41] Gesetz zur Durchführung des Europäischen Übereinkommens vom 20. Mai 1980 über die Anerkennung und Vollstreckung von Entscheidungen über das Sorgerecht für Kinder und die Wiederherstellung des Sorgerechts, [Act to Implement the European Convention on Recognition and Enforcement of Decisions concerning Custody of Children and on Restoration of Custody of Children] [Act to Implement the European Convention], art. 1, LGBL 1997, No. 24. Contact information for the government of the Principality of Liechtenstein is available at http://www.regierung.li/contact.

[42] Convention on the Rights of the Child, opened for signature Nov. 20, 1989, entered into force Sept. 2, 1990, 1577 U.N.T.S. 3.

[43] KINDER- UND JUGENDGESETZ [KJG] [ACT ON CHILDREN AND ADOLESCENTS], LGBL 2009, No. 29.

Dienste) is designated as the central authority for children and adolescents and given a prominent role in discharging the duties of the KJG.

As to legal aid, article 5, paragraph 1 of the Act to Implement the European Convention[44] provides that the central authority (i.e. the government) forwards the application from a foreign applicant to the Regional Court (*Landgericht*). According to paragraph 2, the head of the Regional Court then appoints a law clerk that works at the Regional Court or an attorney according to section 67 of the Rules of Civil Procedure[45] to represent the applicant. In general, legal aid and the appointment of an attorney are dependent on the financial circumstances of the applicant and the likelihood of success of the application.[46] Whether the appointment of a law clerk is also dependent on these factors is not clear from the wording of the law. If the application for return of the child is denied, the court grants legal aid and appoints an attorney without regard to the general requirements (financial circumstances and likelihood of success) in order to file an appeal.[47] In cases of an improper removal, the court is obligated to involve the Office of Social Affairs for the return of the child.[48]

According to the Office of Social Affairs, within the government, the Office for Foreign Affairs (Amt für Auswärtige Angelegenheiten),[49] which forms part of the Ministry for Foreign Affairs, Education and Culture (Ministerium für Äusseres, Bildung und Kultur), would be the contact point for applicants from countries that are not parties to the European Convention.[50]

Moldova

The Republic of Moldova became an independent state of the former Soviet Union on August 27, 1991.[51] The Constitution of the Republic of Moldova and the Family Code of the Republic of Moldova determine the basic principles regarding family relations and child protection. The Constitution declares that the state must protect the family[52] and obligates parents to ensure their children's upbringing, education, and training.[53] According to the Family Code, all family-

---

[44] Act to Implement the European Convention, LGBL1997, No. 24.

[45] Zivilprozessordnung [ZPO] [Rules of Civil Procedure], LGBL 1912, No. 9/1.

[46] ZPO, § 63, ¶ 1.

[47] Act to Implement the European Convention, art. 5, ¶ 3.

[48] *Id.* art. 5, ¶ 4.

[49] *Amt für Auswärtige Angelegenheiten* [*Office for Foreign Affairs*], LANDESVERWALTUNG FÜRSTENTUM LIECHTENSTEIN, http://www.llv.li/#/114773/english-version (last visited May 4, 2015).

[50] Email from Ludwig Frommelt, Head of the Office of Social Affairs, Liechtenstein National Administration, to Law Library of Congress Foreign Law Specialist (Apr. 24, 2015, 4:53 AM) (on file with Foreign Law Specialist).

[51] *Moldova, in* CIA WORLD FACTBOOK, https://www.cia.gov/llibrary/publications/the-world-factbook/geos/md.html (last updated Apr. 21, 2015).

[52] CONSTITUTION OF THE REPUBLIC OF MOLDOVA art. 48, July 29, 1994, *as amended*, http://legislationline.org/documents/action/popup/id/16261/preview.

[53] *Id.*

related disputes are to be adjudicated by the local district court where one of the spouses permanently resides.[54]

It appears that parental abduction is treated by Moldova's family legislation as a form of child abuse committed by a parent or a person replacing the parent. In such cases, a parent whose rights are violated or the child involved can independently apply for protection of his/her rights and legitimate interests to the Guardianship Authority, which is a part of Moldova's Ministry of Labor, Family, and Social Protection, or to a court. A child can petition a court upon reaching the age of fourteen.[55]

The Guardianship Authority is the government institution authorized to resolve disputes in cases of parental abduction.[56] According to media reports, documents issued by the Ministry are accepted by foreign courts making decisions in cases where children have been illegally taken to Moldova by one of the parents.[57] While no information was located about formal legal representation domestically and abroad in parental abduction cases, it appears that the national office of the People's Advocate (Ombudsman) for Children Rights Protection provides legal assistance to parents whose custody rights have been violated.[58] According to the Ombudsman, twenty-eight children have been removed illegally from Moldova in the last five years.[59]

The Criminal Code of the Republic of Moldova, adopted on April 18, 2002, does not recognize parental abduction as a crime. However, the Code states that the abduction of a child by a close relative is a crime punishable by a fine, community service for a period of up to 240 days, or six months' imprisonment.[60] Removing a child from the country or retaining a child outside of Moldova without parental permission is punishable by two to six years' imprisonment.[61]

Special procedures were instituted in 1994 for minors to cross the national border. According to the Law on Exit from and Entry into the Republic of Moldova, minors have the right to leave and enter the Republic of Moldova only if accompanied by a legal representative or an accompanying person designated in a notarized declaration by the legal representative. The

---

[54] FAMILY CODE OF THE REPUBLIC OF MOLDOVA, Law No. 1316-XIV, art. 53, Oct. 26, 2000, http://lex.justice.md/ru/286119/ (in Russian).

[55] *Id.*

[56] Statute on the Ministry of Social Protection, Family, and Child, Law No. 357-XVI, Nov. 24, 2006, MONITORUL OFICIAL (official gazette) Dec. 8, 2006, No. 186 (in Romanian). More information on Moldovan national activities in the field of children rights protection can be found in the annual Social Protection Reports published in English by the Ministry on its website, at http://mpsfc.gov.md/en/rapoarte/ (last visited Apr. 28, 2015).

[57] *Ombudsman: Kidnapping Children in Moldova Becomes Alarming*, TELERADIO MOLDOVA (Jan. 14, 2015), http://www.trm.md/en/social/ombudsman-rapirea-copiilor-din-republica-moldova-devine-un-fenomen-alarmant.

[58] Law No. 52 on the People's Advocate (Ombudsman) art. 1.7, Apr. 3, 2014, http://ombudsman.md/sites/default/files/legislatie/legea_ombudsman_52_engl.pdf.

[59] TELERADIO MOLDOVA, *supra* note 57.

[60] CRIMINAL CODE OF THE REPUBLIC OF MOLDOVA, Law No. 985-XV, art. 164, Apr. 18, 2002, http://lex.justice md/ru/331268/ (in Russian).

[61] *Id.* art. 207.

declaration must specify the purpose of the trip, its duration, and the country of destination.[62] For children between the ages of ten and eighteen traveling abroad to establish permanent residence, the Law requires their written consent expressed in a declaration containing the child's notarized signature.[63] If one of the parents of a child under eighteen years of age does not consent to the child's departure, the parent's denial may be appealed to a local court of general jurisdiction.[64]

III. Latin America and the Caribbean

Antigua and Barbuda

Antigua and Barbuda, while not a party to the Hague Convention on the Civil Aspects of International Child Abduction, is a party to a regional convention, the Inter-American Convention on the International Return of Children.[65] That Convention provides a mechanism for cooperation between countries for the return of children who have been wrongfully removed from one State Party to another.[66] Antigua and Barbuda has appointed the office of the Attorney General as its central authority under the Convention.[67]

The Convention provides that "[c]osts of the return [of the child] shall be borne by the claimant; should the claimant lack the means, the authorities of a requesting State may defray the costs, which may be recovered from the person responsible for the wrongful removal or retention."[68] It is unclear what types of costs are included under this provision.

At the domestic level, family disputes, such as divorce and child custody, are adjudicated in both the Magistrates Court and the High Court.[69] The court may include in any custody order a term that requires the person with custody of the child to notify any person granted access to the child any intention of changing residence at least thirty days in advance.[70]

The requirements of consent for a minor to obtain a passport in Antigua and Barbuda vary according to the marital status of the parents. If the parents are married, the father must provide

---

[62] Law on Exit and Entry into the Republic of Moldova, No. 269-XIII, art. 1.2, Nov. 9, 1994, http://lex.justice md/index.php?action=view&view=doc&lang=2&id=311638 (in Russian).

[63] *Id.* art. 3.3.

[64] *Id.* art. 3.5.

[65] Inter-American Convention on the International Return of Children, July 15, 1989, 29 I.L.M. 63 (1990), http://www.oas.org/juridico/english/treaties/b-53.html.

[66] *Id.* art. 1.

[67] Organization of American States, Inter-American Convention on the International Return of Children, Signatories and Ratifications, http://www.oas.org/juridico/english/sigs/b-53.html (last visited May 5, 2015).

[68] Inter-American Convention, *supra* note 65, art. 13.

[69] Magistrate's Code of Procedure Act 1892, cap. 255 § 121, http://www.laws.gov.ag/acts/chapters/cap-255.pdf; Divorce Act 1997, No. 10 of 1997, § 14, http://www.laws.gov.ag/acts/1997/a1997-10.pdf.

[70] Divorce Act 1997, No. 10 of 1997, § 14(7), http://www.laws.gov.ag/acts/1997/a1997-10.pdf.

written consent, and in cases where the parents are not married, only the consent of the mother is required.[71]

The Constitution of Antigua and Barbuda does not specify that legal aid will be provided to any person in civil cases,[72] nor is there any law that specifically provides for a system of legal aid or assistance. A project for legal aid was established in August 2003 following concern over the lack of legal aid in the country; however, no provision has yet been made for legal aid in civil matters.[73]

Aruba[74]

No provisions were found in Aruban law that specifically deal with the issue of international parental child abductions. However, the Civil Code of Aruba has certain provisions that might be relevant to the handling of such cases. For example, the Code provides that where the parents exercise joint parental authority, disputes between them in respect of that authority are to be submitted at the request of both or one of them to the court of first instance. Before deciding, the court must first attempt to reach an agreement between the parents, and in taking any decision, the court must act in the best interests of the child.[75] In addition, there are Criminal Code provisions that address the crimes of cross-border kidnapping[76] and intentional withdrawal of a minor from a lawful authority.[77]

Legal aid for both criminal and civil matters is provided in conformity with the National Ordinance on Free Legal Assistance.[78] In order to receive legal aid, a party to a legal dispute must apply for a card for legal assistance (CLA), by first obtaining a CLA appointment form from the Free Legal Assistance section of the Social Affairs Department (Directie Sociale

---

[71] *Application for Antigua and Barbuda Passport for Applicants Under 16*, GOV.AG, http://www.forms.gov.ag/passport/application_form_teen.pdf (last visit April 28, 2015).

[72] Antigua and Barbuda Constitution Order 1981, cap. 23, 1 LAWS OF ANTIGUA AND BARBUDA (rev. ed. 1992).

[73] *Cardiff's Legal Skills Spread to Antigua*, CARDIFF LAW SCHOOL, http://www.law.cf.ac.uk/alumni/newsletter/2005/jul/july8.html (last visited Apr. 28, 2015).

[74] At present there are no Law Library of Congress research staff members versed in Dutch. This report has been prepared based on practiced legal research methods and on the basis of relevant legal resources, chiefly in English, currently available in the Law Library and online.

[75] LANDSVERORDENING bevattende de tekst van Boek 1 voor een nieuw Burgerlijk Wetboek van Aruba, AB 2001 no. 89, *last amended by* AB 2012 no. 54 (implemented by AB 2013 no. 15), http://www.overheid.aw/document.php?m=7&fileid=8703&f=24ddda754d93d52e8e45c404459987f3&attachment=0&c=10951.

[76] LANDSVERORDENING van 27 april 2012 houdende vaststelling van een nieuw Wetboek van Strafrecht van Aruba [Wetboek van Strafrecht van Aruba], AB 2012 No. 24, *last amended by* AB 2014 No. 11 (in force by AB 2014 No. 12), art. 2: 245, http://www.overheid.aw/document.php?m=7&fileid=17393&f=5b1491b6f8298bd06ec1090332c028d1&attachment=0&c=13435.

[77] *Id.* arts. 2:246 & 2:247.

[78] Landsverordening kosteloze rechtskundige bijstand [Landsverordening kosteloze rechtskundige bijstand] [National Ordinance on Free Legal Assistance], AB 1991 No. GT 45, *last amended by* AB [AFKONDIGINGSBLAD VAN ARUBA] 1997 No. 34, http://www.overheid.aw/document.php?m=7&fileid=8325&f=7430ed249729ba1f5384b0c6d9d7fc37&attachment=0&c=10457.

Zaken).[79] The CLA appointment form is used to obtain required documents from the Population Register to prove Aruban residency and one's income statement, which are then submitted to the Social Affairs Department on the date of the appointment.[80]

The CLA application is assessed by the Free Legal Assistance section of the Social Affairs Department based on the following criteria: possession of Dutch nationality residence or resident alien status; the nature of the conflict, e.g., being between persons and being civil law cases, personal and/or family law cases, or criminal cases; the amount of income and/or property to determine if the person is someone with insufficient or limited means; and the substance of the case.[81]

According to the National Ordinance on Free Legal Assistance, foreign nonresidents who meet the Ordinance's requirements may be eligible for legal aid in criminal cases. To the extent that an international agreement exists between Aruba and the relevant foreign jurisdiction, a foreigner may also be eligible for free legal assistance in civil matters.[82] A National Decree adopted in connection with the Criminal Procedure Law contains additional legal aid provisions and establishes a commission to formulate relevant guidelines.[83]

Bolivia

Bolivia is a party to the Inter-American Convention on the International Return of Children.[84] The Convention applies to the return of children wrongfully removed from one State Party to the Convention to another.[85]

According to the Convention, the Central Authority designated by each party member assists the applicant and competent authorities of the respective states in locating and returning children.[86] It is also in charge of assuring the prompt return and delivery of the child to the applicant and

---

[79] *Legal System and Free Legal Assistance*, ARUBA BAR ASSOCIATION, http://www.ova.aw/index.php?option= com_content&view=article&id=4&Itemid=7&lang=en (last visited Apr. 28, 2015). In Dutch, the card is referred to as *kaart rechtgevende op kosteloze rechtsbijstand aanvragen* (KRB). *See also* National Ordinance on Free Legal Assistance art. 2, ¶ 1.

[80] ARUBA BAR ASSOCIATION, *supra* note 79.

[81] *Id.*

[82] National Ordinance on Free Legal Assistance art. 2, ¶ 2.

[83] LANDSBESLUIT, houdende algemene maatregelen, ter uitvoering van enkele artikelen van het Wetboek van Strafvordering van Aruba (AB 1996 No. 75) inzake de verlening van toevoegingen in strafzaken [Landsbesluit toevoeging in strafzaken] [National Decree, Lay3ing Down General Measures for the Implementation of Some Articles of the Code of Criminal Procedure of Aruba on the Grant of Requests in Criminal Matters [National Decision on Requests in Criminal Matters], AB 1997 No. 50, http://www.gobierno.aw/document.php?m=15&fileid= 13046&f=b66ae54bee9dee8befc16311cc280b6b&attachment=0&c=18370.

[84] Inter-American Convention, *supra* note 65.

[85] *Id.* art. 1; *Signatories and Ratifications, Inter-American Convention on the International Return of Children*, ORGANIZATION OF AMERICAN STATES (OAS), http://www.oas.org/juridico/english/sigs/b-53.html (last visited May 5, 2015).

[86] Inter-American Convention, *supra* note 65, art. 7, ¶ 2.

assisting the parties in obtaining the necessary documents for proceedings required under the Convention.[87] Bolivia has designated the Deputy Minister of Youth, Children and the Elderly as its central authority under the Convention.[88]

The Convention provides that costs incurred for the return are borne by the claimant, but that if he or she cannot afford them, the authorities of a requesting State may defray the costs, which may be later recovered from the person responsible for the wrongful removal or retention of the child.[89]

The processing of letters rogatory or requests and measures related to the restitution proceedings under the Convention are free of charge and exempt from any type of tax, deposit, or bond.[90]

Cuba

No information was located as to whether Cuba provides any form of legal assistance to a parent whose child was abducted to or from the country. Also, no information was located to indicate whether there is an agency that handles legal representation for such parents.

Guyana

The laws of Guyana do not require the provision of legal representation to a child abducted to or from the country. It also does not appear to have a designated agency for handling legal representation in cases involving parental abductions.

No Guyanese laws providing for legal aid services were identified.

Haiti

No information was located as to whether Haiti provides any form of legal assistance to a parent whose child was abducted to or from the country. Also, no information was located indicating whether there is an agency that handles legal representation for such parents.

Haiti has signed but not ratified the Inter-American Convention on the International Return of Children.[91]

---

[87] *Id.* art. 7.

[88] *Signatories and Ratifications*, OAS, *supra* note 85.

[89] Inter-American Convention, *supra* note 65, art. 13.

[90] *Id.* art. 23, ¶ 1.

[91] Organization of American States, Inter-American Convention on the International Return of Children, Signatories and Ratifications, http://www.oas.org/juridico/english/sigs/b-53.html (last visited May 5, 2015).

Jamaica

The laws of Jamaica do not require the provision of legal representation to a child abducted to or from these countries. The country also does not seem to have a designated agency for the handling of legal representation in cases involving parental abductions. Under Jamaican law, however, affected parties may receive legal representation from legal aid authorities. According to Jamaica's Legal Aid Act, "[s]ave in relation to an excepted matter or proceeding, legal aid may be granted to any person who (a) is in need of legal services in any civil cause or matter." [92]

Saint Lucia

The laws of Saint Lucia do not require legal representation in the case of a child abducted to or from the country. It also does not appear to have a designated agency for handling legal representation in cases involving parental abduction. Under Saint Lucia's laws, however, affected parties may receive legal representation from legal aid authorities.

Saint Lucia's Legal Aid Act 2007 provides that "[a] person who cannot afford to obtain legal services from a private attorney at law may apply to the Board [of the Authority appointed under section 3 of the Act] for legal aid." [93]

Saint Vincent and the Grenadines

Saint Vincent and the Grenadines has a Family Court that handles family law issues. [94] Custody is determined in accordance with the provisions of the Law of Minors Act 1989. [95] Some national laws restrict parents in removing their children from the country. Specifically, section 22 of the Law of Minors Act provides that the court may include a provision in a custody order that restricts parents from removing their children out of Saint Vincent and the Grenadines. [96]

Legal aid is currently only provided to indigent defendants charged with a capital offense. [97] Legal assistance is provided to indigent victims in Saint Vincent through nongovernment organizations (NGOs). This assistance appears to be available primarily for victims of human rights violations—for example, through the St. Vincent and the Grenadines Human Rights Association. [98] This Association has stated that no legal clinics exist in St. Vincent, but that the

---

[92] Legal Aid Act No. 36, 1997, *as amended*, §16, JAMAICA MINISTRY OF JUSTICE, http://moj.gov.jm/sites/default/files/laws/Legal%20Aid%20Act_1.pdf.

[93] Legal Aid Act 2007, §§ 31 & 2, SAINT LUCIA ACTS AND STATUTORY INSTRUMENTS, Act No. 6 (2008).

[94] Family Court Act 1992, No. 53 of 1992.

[95] Law of Minors Act 1989 cap. 232, § 12.

[96] *Id.* § 22.

[97] CONSTITUTION OF SAINT VINCENT AND THE GRENADINES (1979), *available at* http://www.wipo.int/wipolex/en/text.jsp?file_id=234369.

[98] *St. Vincent and the Grenadines*, STETSON UNIVERSITY, http://www.stetson.edu/law/international/caribbean/home/media/ACLI-st-vincent.pdf (last visited Apr. 21, 2015).

government provides funding and building space to local NGOs that provide services to indigent victims.[99]

A 2004 news report stated that the government was considering the implementation of a more robust system of legal aid,[100] and a proposed Constitution in 2009, which was later defeated, included a provision to grant legal aid to more individuals.[101] The constitutional amendment would have provided legal assistance to "accused indigent persons . . . subjected to capital punishment, as well as in other cases where such persons face serious criminal charges if in such cases legal aid is recommended by the presiding judicial officer."[102] No legal aid appears to be available for civil cases.

IV. Middle East and North Africa

Iran

Iran substantially reverted to Sharia Laws after the 1979 Islamic Revolution. The Iranian Islamic Penal Code recognizes abduction as the equivalent of kidnapping, which requires a criminal *mens rea* that is not available in a case of illegal removal of a child by a parent.[103] The terminology of "parental abduction" does not exist in Iranian laws; nevertheless, hampering custody orders by one of the parents or a third party has civil and criminal aspects punishable by punitive damages and imprisonment.[104]

Private law matters, including family law, are governed by the Iranian Constitution,[105] Civil Code,[106] and various acts, laws, and regulations. If, due to separation, divorce, or other reasons, parents are not living in the same residence, the noncustodial parent should be granted visitation

---

[99] *Id.*

[100] *Legal Aid to Be Implemented Soon in St Vincent*, CARIBBEAN NEWS (Feb. 6, 2004), http://www.caribbean newsnow.com/topstory-Legal-aid-to-be-implemented-soon-in-St-Vincent-234.html.

[101] Saint Vincent and the Grenadines Constitution Act 2009, art. 9, *available at* http://www.hsph.harvard.edu/ population/womenrights/stvincent.constitution.09.pdf. Note that, although passed by the House of Assembly, this proposed Constitution was defeated in a referendum and never entered into force.

[102] *Id.*

[103] QANUN-I MOJAZAAT ISLA'MAI [ISLAMIC PENAL CODE] Tehran 1370 [1991] art. 621, *available at* http://iranhrdc.org/english/human-rights-documents/iranian-codes/1000000351-islamic-penal-code-of-the-islamic-republic-of-iran-book-five.html (in English).

[104] QANUN-I MADANI [CIVIL CODE] Tehran 1376 [1997] arts. 1174, 1175, *available at* http://www.alaviand associates.com/documents/civilcode.pdf (in English); ISLAMIC PENAL CODE art. 632; Law of 13 July 1986 (Custody Right Law – Single Clause), *available at* http://www.sabteahval.ir/Upload/Modules/Contents/asset81/hag hehezanat.pdf (in Farsi).

[105] QANUN-I ASSASI JUMHURI ISLA'MAI IRAN [CONSTITUTION OF THE ISLAMIC REPUBLIC OF IRAN] 1358 [1980] arts. 10, 12, 13, 21, *available at* http://en.parliran.ir/index.aspx?fkeyid=&siteid=84&pageid=3054 (in English).

[106] CIVIL CODE arts. 956–1257.

rights at least once per month.[107] A parent cannot and should not be deprived of his/her custody or visitation rights, unless due to a legal necessity, and by a court order.[108] The Family Court, also known as the Special Civil Court,[109] has jurisdiction to resolve cases related to custody rights.[110]

A parent who has been granted custody, or a qualified third party who has custody, cannot remove the child from the city/province and country where the child resides, unless the other parent gives written permission or there is a court order.[111] The Iranian Custody Clause of 1986 considers hindering a custody order by illegally removing or retaining the child a crime punishable by detention and punitive damages until the offending party fully complies with the order.[112] The Iranian Islamic Penal Code establishes a separate penalty of three to six months of imprisonment or a fine of 500,000 to 3,000,000 Rials for a person who interferes with custody or visitation arrangements by retention of the child.[113]

Criminal penalties related to custody matters can be enforced upon petition of one of the parties who has standing.[114] The Family Court is the central authority to evaluate, verify, and enforce foreign custody awards issued by foreign courts or arbitrators.[115] Family Courts also have jurisdiction to hear criminal matters arising from custody issues.[116] Parties are able to designate arbitrators with the court's permission, and/or if the court decides to proceed via arbitration.[117]

In contrast with the foregoing criminal removal or retention of children by their parents, the Penal Code considers child abduction the equivalent of kidnapping of children by force, deceit, or other methods, which is punishable by fifteen years of imprisonment for victims younger than fifteen, and five to fifteen years of imprisonment for victims over fifteen. The Iranian Supreme

---

[107] *Id.* art. 1174; A'innameh Ijrai Qanun-i Hemayat Khanevadeh Shomareh 2654 [Family Protection Law Executive Regulations No. 2654] Tehran 1354 [1975] art. 12, *in* RUZNA'MEH-I RASMI JUMHURI ISLA'MAI IRAN [OFFICIAL GAZETTE OF THE ISLAMIC REPUBLIC OF IRAN], Family Protection Law Executive Regulations, 21 May 1975–8846.

[108] CIVIL CODE art. 1175.

[109] Layeheh Qanuni-i Tashkil Daadgah Madani Khaas [Statutory Instrument for Establishment of Special Civil Court] Tehran 1358 [1979] arts. 1, 3, 8, 15, 17, *in* RUZNA'MEH-I RASMI JUMHURI ISLA'MAI IRAN, Statutory Instrument for Establishment of Special Civil Court, 11 Oct. 1979–10088.

[110] Qanun-i Hemayat Khanevadeh [Family Protection Law] Tehran 1353 [1975] arts. 1, 14 *available at* https://tavaana.org/sites/default/files/family_protection_act.pdf (in Farsi).

[111] *Id.* art. 14, amend. 1.

[112] Law of 13 July 1986 (Custody Right Law – Single Clause), *available at* http://www.sabteahval.ir/Upload/Modules/Contents/asset81/haghehezanat.pdf (in Farsi).

[113] ISLAMIC PENAL CODE art. 632.

[114] Family Protection Law art. 22.

[115] Qanun-i Ijrai Ahkam Madani [Executive Law for Civil Judgments] Tehran 1356 [1977] arts. 169, 170, 177, 178, *in* RUZNA'MEH-I RASMI JUMHURI ISLA'MAI IRAN, Executive Law for Civil Judgments, 20 Sept. 1977–9610; Family Protection Law art. 7, amend.; A'INI DADRASSI'I MADANI [CIVIL PROCEDURE CODE] Tehran 1379 [2000], ch. 2, art. 31, 32, *available at* http://www.ghanoonbaz.com/anavin/Madani/Aeindadresi_Madani/aeinedadresi_madani1.htm.

[116] Statutory Instrument for Establishment of Special Civil Court art. 3, § 5.

[117] Family Protection Law arts. 5, 6, 8.

Court Consultancy Committee has interpreted the elements of this law to include a criminal *mens rea*, such as demanding money, lucrative favors, and taking revenge, and excluding any other form of removal that does not carry the same criminal intent.[118] If abduction or kidnapping leads to other crimes, such as assault, rape, physical injury, or death of the victim, the penalties can be elevated up to the death penalty, depending on the gravity of the harm and the age of the victim.[119]

The permission of a child's guardian—or, where necessary, a court order—is required to obtain a passport or to include the child in a qualified relative's passport as a minor traveler.[120] The removal of a child to a foreign country without a legitimate passport or by a passport that has been acquired through fraud is a punishable crime under the jurisdiction of the public courts, or the family courts if directly related to a family case or order.

If a child is abducted to Iran in violation of a foreign custody order and that foreign order is already registered at the Iranian Consulate, the enforcement process and investigations can begin immediately. A petition to a family court or public court of first instance can be filed through the Iranian consulate in the foreign country of the main residence or directly at a court in the place of residence of the child or respondent in Iran; if the exact residence in Iran is unknown in Tehran, the petition may be filed in Tehran.[121] This may be done in person or by proxy.[122] If there is a foreign criminal order related to an abduction matter other than illegal removal or retention of a child due to a custody conflict, the parties can file a motion through the International Division of the Ministry of Justice to grant jurisdiction to Iranian authorities to investigate, evaluate, and enforce legal proceedings, and to cooperate with Interpol.[123]

Iran generally assists with accepting foreign judgments after verifying that another alternative judgment from an Iranian court does not exist, that the judgment is in compliance with the public order of the country, treaties, and bilateral agreements,[124] and that it is final and valid. In criminal matters, Iran cooperates with Interpol if the written application to the International Division of the Ministry of Justice is approved. The level of assistance and cooperation with another country is governed by bilateral agreements with that country. Presently, Iran has bilateral agreements in matters of private law with Iraq, Kuwait, and Syria.[125]

---

[118] Supreme Court of the Islamic Republic of Iran, [Case Name Unknown], 18 Mar. 1996, 74/2287, *available at* http://www.ghavanin.ir/detail.asp?id=5125.

[119] Qanun-i Tashdid Mojazat Robayandegan-i Ashkhas [Aggravated Penalty Law for Kidnappers] Tehran 1353 [1975], *available at* http://www.dastour.ir/brows/?lid=%20%20%20%20%2085928.

[120] Qanun-i Gozarnaameh [Passport Law] arts. 21, 22, 23, *available at* http://ravash.ir/pages/view/pageid/155/lang/fa (last visited Apr. 30, 2015).

[121] Family Protection Law art. 7.

[122] Family Protection Law Executive Regulations No. 2654, art. 2, amend.; CIVIL PROCEDURE CODE ch. 2, arts. 31 & 32.

[123] Forms available on the website of the International Division of the Ministry of Justice, at http://www.bia-judiciary.ir/Default.aspx?tabid=3657 (last visited Apr. 28, 2015).

[124] Executive Law for Civil Judgments art. 171.

[125] List of Bilateral Agreements, INTERNATIONAL DIVISION OF THE MINISTRY OF JUSTICE, http://www.bia-judiciary.ir/Default.aspx?tabid=3670 (in Persian; last visited Apr. 28, 2015).

Saudi Arabia

No information was located as to whether Saudi Arabia provides any form of legal assistance to a parent whose child was abducted to or from the country. Also, no information was located indicating whether there is an agency handling legal representation for such parents.

Tunisia

No information was located as to whether Tunisia provides any form of legal assistance to a parent whose child was abducted to or from the country. Also, no information was located indicating whether there is an agency handling legal representation for such parents.

V. South Asia

India

India's Legal Services Authorities Act[126] establishes statutory bodies called legal services authorities "to give effect to the policies and directions"[127] of India's National Legal Services Authority (NALSA) in the states of India and "to provide free and competent legal services to the weaker sections of the society to ensure that opportunities for securing justice are not denied to any citizen by reason of economic or other disabilities."[128] The criteria for granting legal aid is established by section 12 of the Act,[129] which states that "[e]very person who has to file or defend a case shall be entitled to legal services under this Act if that person is . . . a woman or a child."[130] The Act provides support to persons in both civil and criminal matters.[131] There do not appear to be any rules regarding legal representation for a parent whose child was abducted from or to India.

Nepal

Nepal's Legal Aid Act[132] authorizes legal aid and the Legal Aid Rules[133] set forth the applicable procedures for legal aid cases. Aid dispensed through the Act is provided by Central and District

---

[126] Legal Services Authorities Act, 1987, No. 39 of 1987, http://nalsa.gov.in/actrules.html.

[127] *Introduction and History of NALSA*, NATIONAL LEGAL SERVICES AUTHORITY (2010), http://nalsa.gov.in/.

[128] Legal Services Authorities Act, preamble.

[129] *Id.*

[130] *Id.* § 12(c).

[131] *Id.* § 2(1)(a).

[132] Legal Aid Act, 2054 (1997), http://www.lawcommission.gov np/site/sites/default/files/Documents/legal-aid-act.pdf.

[133] Legal Aid Rules, 2055 (1998), http://www.lawcommission.gov.np/site/sites/default/files/Documents/Legal%2B Aid%2BRules%2C%2B2055.pdf.

Legal Aid Committees (DLACs).[134]   The Act and the Rules authorize the provision of legal aid when the person has less than a "specified annual income,"[135] which is currently NPR40,000 (about US$390) and below.[136]   The Act does not appear to distinguish between civil and criminal matters.   Provisions on legal aid are also found in the Supreme Court Rules, Appellate Court Rules, and District Court Rules.[137]   No information was located concerning specifically tailored rules regarding legal representation for a parent whose child was abducted from or to Nepal.

Pakistan

Rules promulgated under Pakistan's Legal Practitioners and Bar Councils Act, 1973[138] provide free legal assistance "to the poor, destitute, orphan, widows, indigent and other deserving litigants"[139] in certain category of "specified civil matters,"[140] which include public interest litigation and family law.[141]   The Pakistan Bar Council is responsible for providing legal aid under the Act.   There do not appear to be any specifically tailored rules regarding legal representation of a parent whose child was abducted from or to Pakistan.   According to a briefing by the Child Rights International Network,

> . . . child victims of crime have the right to free legal assistance at the expense of the Government.   The Government has also established the Public Defender and Legal Aid Office to provide legal assistance to indigent persons involved in criminal proceedings, and any person interested in the welfare of a child may seek legal assistance from the Office on behalf of that child.[142]

VI. Sub-Saharan Africa

Cameroon

No information was located as to whether Cameroon provides any form of legal assistance to a parent whose child was abducted to or from the country.   Also, no information was located indicating whether there is an agency handling legal representation for such parents.

---

[134] USAID, STUDY OF THE CURRENT LEGAL AID SYSTEM IN NEPAL (Sept. 2, 2005), http://pdf.usaid.gov/pdf_docs/PNADJ826.pdf.

[135] Legal Aid Act § 3(1).

[136] Legal Aid Rules § 6(1).

[137] USAID, *supra* note 134, at 16.

[138] Legal Practitioners & Bar Councils Act, 1973, No. 35, http://www.pbbarcouncil.com/downloads/barcouncil_act_amended_2005.pdf.

[139] Pakistan Bar Council Free Legal Aid Rules, 1999, § 3(a), http://pakistanbarcouncil.org/wp-content/uploads/2012/07/1999.pdf.

[140] Child Rights International Network, *Legal Briefing on Children's Rights in Pakistan*, https://www.crin.org/docs/Pakistan_Legal_Status_Final.pdf (last visited Apr. 29, 2015).

[141] Pakistan Bar Council Free Legal Aid Rules § 3(a)(iii) & (viii).

[142] Child Rights International Network, *supra* note 140.

Cape Verde

Cape Verde does not appear to have a specific provision or government program designed to provide legal representation in cases involving the abduction of a child in the country or abroad, or a designated agency in charge of handling legal representation regarding parental abduction of children. It was not possible to determine whether the government of Cape Verde makes available to its citizens any type of legal assistance concerning parental abduction of children.

Equatorial Guinea

No information was located as to whether Equatorial Guinea provides any form of legal assistance to a parent whose child was abducted to or from the country. Also, no information was located indicating whether there is an agency handling legal representation for such parents.

Kenya

Kenya does not appear to have legislation or a government program that provides for legal aid in cases involving parental abduction of children. This is true both in situations where children are abducted from Kenya or abducted abroad and brought into Kenya. A search of the Law Library of Congress collection on Kenya and online searches yielded no results.

Mozambique

Mozambique does not appear to have a dedicated agency or office that provides legal representation in cases involving the abduction of a child in the country or abroad, and there is no specific office responsible for providing legal representation in cases involving parental abduction of children. It was not possible to determine whether the government of Mozambique makes available to its citizens any type of legal assistance concerning parental abduction of children.

Nigeria

Nigeria does not appear to have a legal aid program aimed specifically at providing legal assistance in cases involving parental abduction of children. This is true both in situations where children are abducted from Nigeria or abducted abroad and brought into Nigeria. Child abduction is a federal offense in Nigeria.[143] Nigeria's Legal Aid Act does not appear to be directly applicable to matters relating to custody or parental abduction; however, it authorizes the country's president to issue regulations for the provision of legal aid with regard to any type of case, which may include custody and abduction matters.[144] No such regulation was located, however.

---

[143] Child Rights Act, 2003, §§ 27 & 47 (July 31, 2003), available on Policy and Legal Advocacy Centre (PLAC) website, *at* http://www.placng.org/new/laws/C50.pdf. This report does not include state laws on the provision of legal aid.

[144] Legal Aid Act, 1977, § 7, 8 LAWS OF THE FEDERATION OF NIGERIA, Cap. L.9 (rev. ed. 2006), *available at* http://www.placng.org/new/laws_of_nigeria3.php?sn=232.

Rwanda

The Rwandan Ministry of Justice has created legal aid offices, called Access to Justice Bureaus or Maisons d'Accès à la Justice (MAJ), in all thirty districts of Rwanda.[145] These offices provide legal information as well as legal advice and mediation services.[146] No information could be located specifically on international child abductions.

São Tomé e Príncipe

São Tomé e Príncipe does not appear to have a program designed to provide legal representation in cases involving the abduction of a child in the country or abroad, or an agency or office in charge of handling legal representation related to parental abduction of children. It was not possible to determine whether the government of São Tomé e Príncipe makes available to its citizens any type of legal assistance concerning parental abduction of children.

Sudan

No information was located as to whether Sudan provides any form of legal assistance to a parent whose child was abducted to or from the country. Also, no information was located indicating whether there is an agency handling legal representation for such parents.

Uganda

Uganda does not appear to have a program specifically designed to provide legal aid in parental abduction cases. This is true both in situations where children are abducted from Uganda or abducted abroad and brought into Uganda. However, a person involved in this type of case may be eligible for assistance under a general law on legal aid. Under this law, a person is eligible for legal aid if, according the assessment of a legal aid provider, he or she is, among other things, indigent and has a reasonable ground for instituting an action and a good prospect of success.[147] This law makes disputes involving domestic violence as well as child maintenance and custody cases among the matters to be given priority when making a determination regarding the provision of legal aid.[148] Legal aid determinations appear to involve a great deal of discretion on the part of the legal aid provider; legal aid does not appear to be available to anyone as a matter of right.

---

[145] Republic of Rwanda Ministry of Justice, *National Legal Aid Policy* (Sept. 2014), at 13, http://www.minijust. gov.rw/fileadmin/Documents/MoJ_Document/Legal_Aid_Policy_-_IMCC_Feedback.pdf.

[146] *Id.*

[147] Advocates (Legal Aid to Indigent Persons) Regulations, 2007, S.I. 12, § 23 (Apr. 5, 2007), available on the Uganda Legal Information Institute (ULII) website, *at* http://www.ulii.org/ug/legislation/statutory-instrument/12.

[148] *Id.* § 25.

www.ingramcontent.com/pod-product-compliance
Lightning Source LLC
Chambersburg PA
CBHW080535190526

45169CB00008B/3171